ACTIONS

Realizing the Power of Your Thoughts

Letizia Florez

CONTENTS

PREFACE

From an early age I began looking for keys to unlock life's mysteries. I sought answers to the common questions.

Why am I here?
Why is this happening?
What is my purpose?
What's the point of all of this?

I searched desperately for meaning and looked everywhere for answers. I read religious books, sought out enlightened individuals, attempted to engage in spiritual practices, but still, I was dumbfounded. I felt so lost in my circumstances that I couldn't see the alternatives.

That is, until life found its own way of revealing the keys. Simply by giving me what I asked for, it revealed the hidden secrets by which we live, yet we may not know we're operating our lives by them. During a crucial moment between life and death, I was propelled on a journey through understanding and transformation. I was showered with a fresh new perspective which served as a launching pad for me to learn how to heal and live a consciously creative life.

As I recount the details of my journey, I take you into my inner world and share intimate details of how the keys revealed themselves. By combining them with my collegiate studies in the fields of psychology, philosophy, and my personal drive toward self-improvement, I discovered techniques that helped me to heal, to rebuild my body and my life.

The keys and techniques that I share with you helped me to develop the ability to direct my thoughts, and thus create the happy and fulfilled life I so desperately yearned for. I have finally realized the feeling of fulfillment I have longed for my entire life and it is my greatest hope that the techniques provided will help you to do the same.

As I have discovered, we are here to remember, acknowledge, embrace, feel, and express our innate and unique greatness. The reason we feel thirsty and incomplete is because we ignore that voice that comes from within and propels us toward our fulfillment. This feeling of fulfillment is not dependent on anything; it is the essence of who we are. We simply have to remember to acknowledge, to accept, to embrace, and to FEEL it. Through this feeling, we are propelled and enabled to express the greatness that wants to express itself through us. Fulfillment is our source of wellbeing and wellbeing is the source from which all great things spring forth.

CHAPTER 1:
DEATH VALLEY ROAD

BZZZ! BZZZZ! BZZZZZ! The alarm clock wakes me out of a deep sleep. It is 4:30 a.m. The call sheet on my nightstand reminds me that I'm shooting my first national commercial in Petaluma, California today. I grab the call sheet which confirms that call time in Petaluma is 6:30 a.m. I jump out of bed and after performing my morning routine, I grab a piece of paper and write a note for my sister. "Sorry baby girl, no minors allowed on the set. I love you." I feel sad as I walk over to the couch where she is sleeping and place it next to her. She was so excited to come with me, I know she will wake up to a huge feeling of disappointment. It would have been her first time on a production set.

It is still dark as I leave Sacramento. 4:30 a.m. is not a strange time to head to the Bay Area for a commercial shoot. I travel eighty-five miles through the usual congested morning traffic and after making the change from Interstate 80 to Highway 37, I turn onto Lakeville Road.

As the sun is just rising, I can see it peeking over the horizon through my rearview mirror. It looks delightful. I'm enthralled with its magic. Lionel Richie's, "Dancing on the Ceiling" is playing on the radio. I'm fully absorbing the mood and lyrics of the song. I tell myself, "It's good to be alive and looking forward to great things."

I look at the clock, it is now 6:20. The production site is about five minutes away, but suddenly my attention is drawn to my driver's side mirror. I notice a pick-up truck coming up on my left. It's attempting to pass me. I'm traveling about sixty-five miles per hour as it is quickly approaching. I slow down a bit and

1

immediately it's on my left. I look up ahead and see a big delivery truck coming out of the curve toward us. My heart races in the grip of adrenaline. I feel it rushing through my body as if it had been shot through my veins. I slow down to let the pick-up truck pass me and get back in the lane, but it's too late. It goes head to head with the delivery truck.

Instantly, I remember my driver's education training during which we were advised not to hit the brakes at high speeds because that will lock the brakes and inevitably throw the car out of control. Instead, I swerve slightly right attempting to dodge the impending collision, while simultaneously trying to avoid the huge Eucalyptus trees lining both sides of the two-lane road. It's a narrow path, but I attempt to squeeze through. As I turn the steering wheel slightly right, I feel a jolt. My car spins out of control and heads straight toward one of the trees. I see the huge tree approaching and hear a horrified scream inside my head, "NO!!! NOT MY FACE!"

CHAPTER 2:
AFTERSHOCK

Everything goes black! It's over. I hear the sounds of crushed metal crackling. The hissing sound of steam consumes the air. The hood of my car is crunched up right in front of my face. The road is quiet. This early in the morning, there are no other cars on the road.

Suddenly, a feeling of desperation overcomes me. My lungs feel obstructed. I can't expand my chest. I'm suffocating. It feels as if I'm being crushed under the weight of something. I glance around for the cause and notice that I'm pinned between the seat and the steering wheel. My heart is racing. I try to stay calm as I perform a point by point damage check of my extremities. Moving ever so slowly, I wiggle my fingers and gently extend my forearms. Trying not to fear the worst, I cautiously and ever so slowly attempt to move my neck from side to side. An incredibly deep sense of relief fills me, as I'm able to move it.

I quickly but carefully reach for the lever on the left side of my seat and pull it. It releases the back of the seat violently taking me with it. I land with an excruciating thud which causes me to take the deep breath I'm yearning for. As I attempt to take in the cool soothing air, I discover that it wasn't the seat squishing me against the steering wheel that was obstructing my breathing; nor was it that the seat was jammed against my ribs. It's ME! There is something wrong with my lungs. I feel like my nose is plugged and I'm trying to breathe through the ultra-thin holes of a miniature coffee stirring straw. The frustration of wanting to breathe and not being able to is suffocating me. I'm getting dizzy.

3

It seems like the harder I try, the more congested and painful my chest feels. I'm getting extremely nervous and my nerves are turning into PANIC. I feel like I'm drowning. I yearn for the feeling of the cool air being pulled in through my nose, traveling down my throat, and deep into the recesses of my expanding rib cage. That familiar feeling I've experienced infinite times before. The longing desire to receive what has always been mine anytime I want has me in its grip.

Suddenly, I understand what a gift it is just to be able to take in a deep breath. How deliciously wonderful just to be able to inhale deeply and savor the cool expansion of my solar plexus. The phrase, "You don't know what you have until it's gone," resounds in my head, as the gift that has always been freely given is now suddenly taken away. How wonderful to be able to breathe any time we want.

Instantly, a memory flashes in my mind of the time my brother shared something he learned in the police academy. He told me that most people die not because of the injuries they sustain, but because they panic. The body goes into shock and shuts down. I immediately resolve to remain calm. I begin to count silently in my mind while attempting to sustain the shallowest of shallow breaths. I feel like I have just the tip of my nose above water, floating on the surface of existence. I'm barely dipping into a tiny bit of air off the top when all I want is to dive into its depths. I'm suffocating and I can do nothing but lay my head back and try to relax.

Then another part of my body screams for attention. The pain in my right foot is throbbing in my shoe. I feel like the Incredible Hulk bursting through the seams. I wish I could reach down and take it off. My left foot is hurting too, but now I become aware that my rib cage and my chest are hurting as well. There is so much pain pulsating throughout my body. Never have I felt this all-encompassing pain before. It's indescribable. All I can do is concentrate intently on escaping it. I want to run from it so badly, I close my eyes and try.

As I attempt to relax, I have a flashback. It is 6 months prior. Images of my reckless drives appear vividly on the screen of my mind. My grandmother had just passed away and I was going through a very painful breakup of a 7 year relationship. As I remember how terrible I felt, it dawns on me that my wish from months ago is being fulfilled. I remember driving passionately angry down the interchange from I-5 to Highway 50. I had the gas "pedal to the metal," while passionately projecting images of a way out in my mind. Deep in my heart, I wished for an escape route. The suffocation from the emotional pain I was experiencing was too intense. I couldn't take it anymore. I fervently coaxed destiny, hoping it would take me with it.

Now, laying in my smashed-up Honda Accord, the realization hits me, "I wished for this. This is what I wished for. My wish came true. This is what I saw in my thoughts while engulfed in emotional pain. I CREATED THIS." A deep sense of sadness and disappointment overcome me as I ask, "Why did I do this to myself?"

I wish I could look outside and see my surroundings but all I can see is the crunched-up hood of the car. I have to rely on my memory. I remember that beyond the grove of trees, all there is to see for miles are golden hay fields and road. My heart sinks as I hear my thoughts, "It's going to take forever for an ambulance to get here and I can't breathe!"

I look at the seat to my right and feel instant relief. It's where my little sister would have been sitting had I not left her at home this morning. I hated disappointing her but all I can think of now is how grateful I am that she isn't here. I've never known such a deep sense of gratitude. It fills me up inside as I lay my head back, close my eyes, and again, try to relax.

CHAPTER 3:
OCEAN OF FACES

As I begin relaxing, I think about my loved ones and how my absence will affect them. I know they will be sad, especially my mom. To say we had hard times while I was growing up is an understatement. I know she will take it hard, but all I can do is hope that in time she'll be okay. I think about my brothers and my sister. I know this will be extremely tough for them, especially after we lost our dad six years ago, to a courageous fight with cancer. I feel completely defeated and hope they will understand. This thought helps me relax and let go. My eyes close as I drift.

I'm in unfamiliar surroundings. Darkness surrounds me. I'm in another world, not a familiar Earthly place. It's definitely not a recognizable physical place. It's as if I'm standing in an open space which extends infinitely around me. I look around and see swirls of cloudy, colorful gases amongst a backdrop of dark blue colored space. I feel a sense of excitement in my gut as if I'm riding down the highest point of a rollercoaster. It's peacefully exhilarating to feel this way, but yet be completely still. I'm in awe of how relaxing it feels to be supported without anything physically solid under me.

Instantly, in front of me appears what I can only describe as an ocean of faces extending as far as my vision allows. They're positioned side by side and one right behind the other, like an enormous audience at a rock concert. Their eye sockets are filled with glowing white light which is being directed straight at me, like millions of flashlight beams. It's difficult to comprehend what I'm looking at. The only way to describe it is to ask you to imagine that you are standing on the beach looking out at the ocean towards the horizon. Imagine that instead of water, you're looking right into countless faces. The light their eyes are reflecting is so luminous and powerful, it's overwhelming. The sudden rush of the realization that they are all looking at me simultaneously, overpowers me. I feel a tremendous force explode against my body and throw me back with an incredibly powerful thrust.

I land some distance back on my behind and immediately look down to check for damages to my body. What I see astounds me. MY BODY IS GONE. I HAVE NO BODY. What I see in its place is a mass of swirling, clear and colorfully transparent, beautifully glowing, radiating particles of LIGHT.

I'm given no time to comprehend this as a deep voice brings me back to the scene of the accident, "Hold on. I called 911. An ambulance is on the way." With strenuous effort, I slightly open my eyes and see the silhouette of a big, tall man standing next to my car, trying to pry the door open. He continues talking but it sounds like buzzing and mumbling. I don't have the energy to try to understand what he is saying. I feel so weak and exhausted that all I want is for him to be quiet. I close my eyes again. It's taking every last drop of energy within me to be calm. I need him to be quiet so I can concentrate on conserving my energy to tolerate the pain, but I can't speak. I long for him to read my mind. "How can he not see that he should be quite in light of the excessive strain I'm under?" He continues. I can't take it anymore, so I figure out the quickest way to get my point across. I signal him with my hand to get close to my mouth. He puts his ear up to it and with the strength I have left, I whisper, "Shut up."

He pulls his head back and with a slightly amused smile keeps talking, "I know you want me to stop talking to you but if I stop, you're going to go to sleep and leave us." He must understand the pleading look in my eyes because he explains, "Life is beautiful.

You're so young. You have so much more to live for. The world needs what you have to give." I'm not really listening. All I can think about is how I long for him to be quiet so I can close my eyes and rest.

Suddenly, we hear the sounds of rustling and voices. The paramedics have arrived. The man steps aside and lets them go right into emergency action. I can't see what's going on but I can hear the voices around me, orders being given and executed. I have always been deathly afraid of needles and here is a paramedic putting one in my arm. It barely matters. Then an oxygen mask appears on my face. It feels obstructive, but then a brace is wrapped tightly around my neck. Now I definitely feel constricted.

Having lost all control of my body and with no idea what is to come, I am forced to surrender for the first time in my life. I have no choice but to let go and have faith in the rescue team's expertise. My only option is to stay in the moment, observe and experience every detail.

A loud buzzing noise startles me as it resounds through the air. I look up and catch a glimpse of what must be what I've heard people call, the "Jaws of Life." It is an intimidating piece of machinery that sounds like a lawn mower and looks like a pair of scissors that are made for a giant. I see them approaching the top frame of the car through the now windowless driver's side door. They grip and lock around the car; I can hear the sharp shrills of metal being torn apart.

I wish I could step away and view the scene from a distance, as I have witnessed so many accidents throughout my life. How nice it would be to be a bystander driving by, believing that accidents only happened to other people. Now, all I can do is imagine what it must look like from afar.

As the roof is pulled up and off of the car, a violent cold wind chill hits me. It's freezing. I feel a cold board being slipped under

9

my back. I'm pulled onto it and the pain instantly intensifies. They're hurting me! The cold board is stuck in the waist of my pants. I grab the closest paramedic's arm and signal him. He immediately shouts to the others to stop. Next thing I know, scissors are slicing straight up each pant leg and up the center of my shirt. In an instant, my clothes are completely gone. The wind chill magnifies and produces goose bumps all over my body. It is unbearable. My breasts feel like they're being pinched down to the nerves. I'm sure I'm going to go insane any minute now. "She's going into shock!" I hear someone yell. The speed at which the paramedics are working multiplies. I hear intensified movements. A blanket is placed over me and I lose track of what's going on.

Searching for a life line, I remember my spiritual studies in which I read that we are one with God and that there is only one God. Without questioning one of our greatest teacher's example, I silently repeat the phrase, "I AND MY FATHER ARE ONE. I AND MY FATHER ARE ONE." I repeat this over and over in my mind. I need to hold on to something to keep my mind from breaking apart. "I and my Father are one. I and my Father are one." I focus all of my attention on repeating the phrase while being pulled out of the car.

The brisk steps of the paramedics signal that we're in motion. We're moving toward the vast golden fields that surround the road. I feel the dry yellow shrubbery scraping against the exposed parts of my bare skin. I concentrate on the phrase while they carry me over a fence, "I AND MY FATHER ARE ONE. I AND MY FATHER ARE ONE." Over and over, I continue to repeat the phrase.

We quickly approach a roaring helicopter with its blades turning full speed. I'm transferred on to it and we immediately take flight. While noisily traveling through the air, I'm desperately holding on to the phrase but it doesn't feel like it's helping much. The vibration and sounds of the chopper are excruciating, not to mention the cold wind that feels like sharp knives slashing painfully through my skin.

So this is what they call, "Life Flight." It's a small two passenger helicopter with just enough room for my gurney, the pilot, and a paramedic. I try to notice more details but all I want is for this ride to come to an end. I try as I hard as I can to keep my mind focused on repeating the phrase. Over and over again it resounds in my mind, "I AND MY FATHER ARE ONE," but the biggest question looming in the foreground is, "Am I going to live through this?"

As soon as we land, a nursing team approaches. They grab the board I'm lying on, place it on top of a gurney, and hurriedly roll it through the long hallways of the hospital. At the end of the long maze, we end up in a room where I'm transferred to a bed. The glorious feeling of the soft mattress conforming itself to my body is not my reward. They lay me down with the hard board under me and explain that they can't take me off of it until they assess the damage. Exasperation overcomes me. I can't take it anymore. I want to scream. It seems like the board is hurting me more than my injuries. How can I possibly endure more pain?

Silent tears well up and roll ever so gently down my cheeks as the feeling of helplessness finally consumes me. I close my eyes and try to calm down. The rest becomes a blur as I'm slid into a big tube that must be a CT scanner.

Finally, the feeling I've been longing for. The soft mattress they just transferred me to is conforming itself to my body. Heaven is the only way I can describe the relief the soft mattress and pillow give me. The anesthesiologist approaches and informs me that they are about to take me into the operating room. He asks me a lot of questions and finalizes them with, "You're going to feel a little drowsy…" He doesn't finish the sentence before I fall into a deep and wonderful sleep.

CHAPTER 4:
DAMAGE REPORT

Strangely, it feels like I wake up instantly. I open my eyes and see a doctor sitting in a chair by my bed, holding my hand and saying, "You're going to be okay." He's looking into my eyes with such compassion and reassurance that I believe him. I feel deeply comforted. He introduces himself as my surgeon and tells me, "You are very lucky to be alive. That was a very dangerous road you were on. People call it, "Death Valley Road" because of the countless number of accidents and deaths that have occurred there. It really helped that you were in such good physical shape. Most people would have died under the circumstances."

Now he delivers the damage report. "You have a metatarsal neck fracture and two fractured ribs, one on each side. The fractures caused your left lung to collapse and your right lung has a contusion." It now makes sense as to why it felt as though I was drowning with every breath I tried to take.

He continues, "Your left foot is fractured and your right foot was crushed." My eyes widen as I exclaim, "CRUSHED? What part?" He responds, "From the ankle down; I put it back together during surgery and used 7 pins to hold it in place." For the first time, I notice that my foot is hanging from a swing like mechanism above my bed wrapped in bloody gauze.

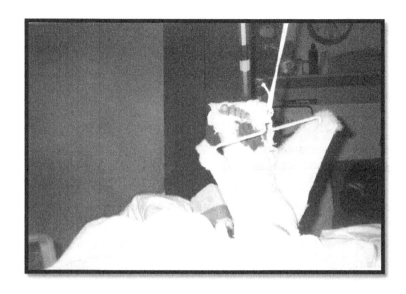

Sadness overcomes me as the results of my previous thoughts are staring right at me. The only thought I can think of now is, "Why did I do this?" Although I didn't cause the accident, I feel a sense of responsibility. I intuitively know I'm no victim but I deeply want to make sense of it all. I am very sad and disappointed with myself as I see my body in this condition.

The doctor continues, "It's going to take a long time for you to walk again. Probably six months to a year and you will always have trouble running and wearing high heels." I exclaim again in shock, "No more high heels? I love high heels!" He gently shakes his head from side to side.

I lay in bed feeling sorry for myself after he leaves my room. I'm full of questions and confusion, but most of all, regret. "What am I going to do now?"

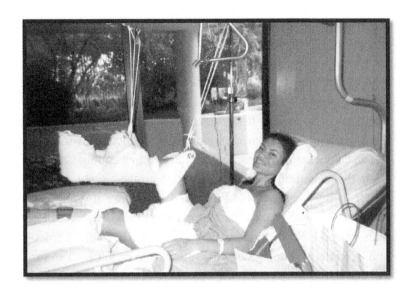

The days that follow are somewhat of a mystery. Everything seems translucent and fluid. Objects that normally look solid, now look as though I can stick my finger right through them. Everything, the wall, the furniture, even the nursing staff seem surreal. I can see through matter in a way I've never seen before. The empty space within and between matter is clearly visible to my naked eyes. It all seems soluble and temporary. I feel as though there's an invisible field surrounding me and if I really want to go through it, I can. It will take me where I long to go. I feel a sense of urgency, as if I need to make a decision quickly because the solubility is only temporary. As if there's a limited time during which this "opening" will be there and then everything will go back to being solid again.

This is a difficult time for me because my family is so far away. I'm in Santa Rosa and everybody I know and love is in Sacramento. It's a two and half hour drive away. This makes it challenging for my family to come immediately, so I don't have any visitors the first day.

The following day, my mother, two brothers, and sister come to visit. They bring a few things for my personal care and needs. We're pleasantly enjoying our visit when severe unexplainable pain sneaks up on me. It skyrockets with no warning. The nurse gave me some pain medication not long before, so I don't understand what's happening. I hit the red light calling her again.

In the meantime, the elder of my two brothers scoots his chair closer to my bed and holds my hand. I squeeze it with all my strength as if with every squeeze I could turn the dial down on the pain. My body is writhing in one giant spasm. The nurse comes in and I go into pleading mode. She refuses and explains, "I'm sorry sweetie but I just gave you the maximum dose for the next hour." My pleading turns into begging. "Please, I just want it to stop. Please, pretty please, just a little bit, please."

She walks towards the door and just as she exits the room, turns around and tells me, "I'll be right back." Mentally relieved but still burning up in pain, I try to control my breathing. My brother continues battling it out with me. I think I'm hurting his hand, but it doesn't seem to matter to him.

The nurse walks back in with a dispenser in her hand, "Excuse me. I'm going to give her this." My brother gets up and takes the only empty chair by the wall. As soon as she gives me the medication, I feel a wonderful surge of warmth migrate through my body. Relief overcomes me as I whisper, "Thank you." I exhale and close my eyes. "She'll be able to sleep now." I hear her say as she exits the room.

Suddenly, I hear a horrified scream, "Hey, she's not sleeping! She's dying!" My mom is in a state of panic. The nurse returns, rapidly assesses me, and instantly slams on the red emergency button by my bed. The light above the door glares red and an extremely loud buzz resounds violently through the entire wing. "CODE BLUE, CODE BLUE!" is being called out over the intercom. An emergency team rushes into my room, surrounds my bed, and goes into immediate action. I see the defibrillator coming toward my chest.

My point of view changes instantly. I feel disoriented and confused. I can see the entire room simultaneously. It's as if I'm floating above my bed just below the ceiling. I see the medical team working on my body. My sister and the younger of my two brothers are asked to step out of the room. I see my other brother sitting in a chair by the wall with his face in his hands. He's in distress. It looks like he's crying. It hurts deeply to see him so vulnerable. I can't bear to see him hurt. His pain consumes me. I long to reach out and reassure him, but I can't.

The medical team continues to work at a rapid pace. A few more pumps and I open my eyes. I'm back in my bed again, exhausted. Immediately, I look for my brother, but I can't see him. I call out to him, "Mijo, don't cry. I'm okay." The crash team's equipment is still surrounding me, blocking my view. He stands up and peers at me above the emergency equipment. He looks slightly confused but simultaneously relieved. The corner of my right cheek curls as I give him a microscopic smile. The emergency team gathers their equipment and one by one exit the room. I feel extremely weak and confused as I ask myself, "Was I just floating above my bed?" I close my eyes as I ponder this question and fall into a deep sleep.

CHAPTER 5:
INTROSPECTION

When I awake, the nurse informs me that my family left a few hours ago. "Your mom thought it would be best for you to rest." A part of me wishes I could be surrounded by my loved ones, yet there's another part of me that welcomes the peace and quiet. It gives me time to reflect on everything that has happened; what series of events led to my experience, and what lies ahead. It feels like somebody has placed a huge brick wall in front of me and I'm standing with my nose right up to it. "What now? Where do I go from here?" The questions are looming over me.

I think about my loved ones, my goals, and my promises. Sometimes, I feel like a spoiled child not able to go out and play. However, as the days wear on, I come to an acceptance that since my wish to exit this world wasn't granted, the only choice I have is to make the best of it. Maybe it means there's a purpose for my continued stay here on Earth. There has to be a reason why I saw the ocean of faces.

Hence, my journey through introspection and self-exploration begins. I feel scared yet strangely excited. During the days that follow there is so much going on in my mind that I feel the need to write it all down. I ask one of the nurses if she can bring me a pen and paper. A few minutes later she walks in with a small pad accompanied with a pen. Poetry begins pouring out of me. I had attempted to write before this moment but suddenly I have so much to say that I don't struggle to form the words. Like a broken water fountain, the words flood the page.

"Thy Will Be Done"

Today I visited a place
That now only exists in time and space
Most would never choose to tread this place
As down a two-lane highway I was going
A quick but costly mistake a young man chose to make
He was too blind to see it wasn't a wise path to take
All I know is that with that move he made
Into his hands he chose my life to take

Right before my eyes, I saw the two trucks collide
As I slightly swerved to the right
I thought my car was out of plight
Little did I know my chances were near to none at all
I felt the shock of the collision
I lost control and my car was on a mission
Right then and there I knew I was involved

Suddenly a life of its own my car seemed to have
As the steering wheel turned itself right out of my hands
I knew my life was in God's hands
Right before the seizure of the motion
I felt the shock of the explosion

20

As almost by a force of nature
I felt the pain in my lungs rupture
As my car had spun right into a tree's direction

As I slammed right into that tree
My Beloved God was the only one I could see
I knew His presence was with me
At that most challenging moment
When there I was
Unable to take in a breath or make any comment
All I could do was lay my head back
And wait for that moment
When all pain would cease
And this world would be nothing more than a memory

Then a vision of my funeral came into my mind
There I saw the faces of all of those I loved
Although tears were in their eyes
As they thought I was nowhere near
I knew in my heart my presence would be in the air
To join in the celebration of my graduation
From this most challenging school we call Life
Where endlessly there seems to be nothing but strife
Then I remembered how young I was

But some of us get to die young

Sadness at the thought of leaving I did not feel
Then, I questioned, "Could this really be real?"
The answer came in a feeling of joyous anticipation
I knew it was time for me to move to the next dimension
But at that very moment into my mind came
All my dreams, all my goals, all my promises
So there I was in such a dilemma
And all I could do was realize
The choice was not mine but my Beloved God's
Then I realized that I and my Creator are One
And for the first time in my life
I turned to my Beloved and said, "Thy will be done"
And laid my head to rest
Seconds after that was said
Help arrived in the form of a man by the name of Will
So I know that I am here by nothing less than God's Will

After this poem pours out of me, I feel a wonderful feeling of satisfaction. I feel grateful to be granted a "vacation" from my responsibilities. I have always wanted time to explore my talents and now I have an abundance of it to explore the world within me. I embrace the opportunity to spend time doing nothing but I silently vow that I will walk within the shortest amount of time possible.

After days of silence, sleep, and deep introspection, I feel like I can simultaneously understand everything. The answers to the questions I've had about my reason for being on Earth and the meaning of life, now seem so obvious. The words of one of our greatest teachers, Jesus the Christ, the teachings of Gautama Buddha, and my early attempts at understanding the Bible become ever so clear.

It suddenly becomes very easy for me to see that our thoughts are the originating point of everything we experience in our lives. Our thoughts create the blueprint for what we will experience. This clarity propels me toward healing and rebuilding my body but it still takes years for me to be able to formulate, in words, the keys that revealed themselves.

A few days into my hospital stay, I have an unexpected visitor. Will, the man who called 911 at the scene of the accident walks in wearing an orthopedic boot. I find it interesting and with a smile I ask, "What happened?" He tells me he hyperextended his ankle while playing basketball the day after my accident. We share our thoughts about our experiences and he hands me this poem.

"Angel"

I helped an angel today
She says I saved her life
From a turn too tight and a flash of light
Her life had changed from day to night

An angel had fallen

Like a bird whose wings were broken

Too hurt to even move

Too weak for words to be spoken

I could not save her with my hands

Or help her with my knowledge

All I could do was comfort her

With a voice to remind her how good life is

She wants to go but she has to stay

Where would we be without her today

A world without an angel

To keep us filled with glee

One less angel in our world

Where in the world would we be

What a sweet blessing to be thought of in this way. I recall whispering to him to "shut up," and needless to say, now, I'm a bit embarrassed. We both laugh as we remember.

After he leaves, I realize that Mother's Day is approaching. I want to do something special for my mom but there isn't much I can do from my bed. I share my thoughts with the nurse, and she suggests I go down to the gift shop and see what they have. Moments later she walks in with a wheelchair and tells me, "The physical therapist will be here soon to show you how to transfer yourself."

It's time for me to leave my room and begin exploring my surroundings, but my new reality hits me. "This is it. This is how I will move around for now. How will I be able to go in public like this? People will stare at me and feel sorry for me." I'm nervous about being noticed and cringe at the attention the chair will inevitably bring.

I become aware of my insecurities and realize how shallow and egotistical I've been. I've relied too heavily on my physical appearance. I've always known that people are visually influenced and I've taken full advantage of that fact. I recall planning the best outfit to get the best results out of every occasion. My motto was, "Always dress for success." I wanted to gain everybody's approval.

Now staring at my new reality, the wheelchair in front of me looks daunting. Instantly, I'm faced with my ego. I hear it whisper, "Just get back under the covers and forget this mess." One part of me wants to listen and avoid the task in front of me but I decide to move forward. My heart is racing as if I'm about to compete in a race.

The physical therapist walks in cheerfully and shows me how to transfer myself. It's a challenge but before I know it, I'm rolling down the hall. My heart beats rapidly. I feel embarrassed and self-conscious but it feels better to be doing this, than to lay in bed. The nurses at the station glance at me with smiles of encouragement as I roll past them and head for the elevator. Once inside, I take advantage of the alone time to calm my nerves. I remember the breathing exercises I learned that help me quiet my thoughts. I breathe in while I silently count to five. I hold my breath while I count to another five, and breathe out while I count to the last five. I learned to do this in even numbered cycles. Holding the breath gives the oxygen time to circulate throughout the blood stream and cleanse the toxins.

I feel nervous excitement and as I reach the first floor, I'm caught like a deer in headlights. I'm immediately faced with the looks I was afraid of. People are looking right at me with obvious questions in their eyes. My instinctive response is to smile cheerfully. They look perplexed as they look down at my legs. They don't know how to respond to my elation. This gives me a tickle and I instantly realize that it doesn't matter what we look like. What matters most is how we feel. Not only is feeling good what we all strive for, but this moment clearly shows me that by choosing thoughts that cause us to feel genuinely good, we automatically have a positive influence on others. We have the power to bring sunshine into the room regardless of what we look like.

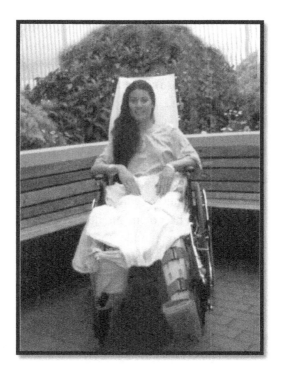

The continued curious glances in my direction help me further understand that a genuine smile, one that comes from joyful thoughts and the joy of being, is the only weapon we have to deflect others' destructive thoughts. It's like an impenetrable piece of armor that protects us. I quickly realize that it's the perfect anecdote to thoughts of pity and misguided concern like, "Poor girl, I wonder what happened to her." This anecdote can be applied to all situations.

Now in the gift store, I notice a lot of beautifully artistic objects but I'm immediately drawn to a light pink colored glass frame with beveled roses. It's the perfect Mother's Day gift, especially since my mother loves roses. It's the next best thing to a dozen real roses. I buy it and take it to my room. Once there, I'm disappointed when I realize that I don't have a picture to put in it. I'm not sure what to do about this so I close my eyes and think of her until I feel her essence.

As I do this, countless thoughts and images spring into my mind. I grew up coveting her approval and affection and because I didn't get it in the way I expected, I felt angry and resentful. As a result of this, we were usually having some sort of conflict. Now laying in my hospital bed, I feel compelled to take out my pen and paper. This time, instead of thinking of all the pain and resentment, I think about all the sacrifices she made to give me a better life. The incredibly difficult decision she made to leave me with my grandparents so she could cross the border from Mexico into California when she was only nineteen years old. The dangers and loneliness she exposed herself to, so she could earn enough money to provide for my needs and education. In the Mexican village where we come from there was very limited free education. Typically, there was one teacher and one classroom for all elementary grades. Even in the nearby city where primary education was accessible, the admission and material costs had to be endured by the families. Therefore, if you came from a poor family, as I did, it was rare to achieve academically and thus grow beyond the social class you were born into.

As I think about the struggles she shared many times with tears in her eyes, I now, allow my heart to really listen to her soul. I think about all the things she did that represented the love she had for me. As I do this, the words begin to flow.

"An Extra-Ordinary Mother"

On this day during which we celebrate our Mothers

I have stopped to think of YOU, my Mother

I've thought about the life you've carried

That your own personal desires for me, you tarried

I've thought about the bridges and borders you crossed

That above all suffering

With an extraordinary strength, you caused

With all this I have come to realize

That you are the mother I one day want to materialize

With all your qualities of strength in handling duress

Your spirit is one that shines with determination and success

Now I sit here with a desire for my love to express

I now know that I am who I am because of your heart's depth

Thinking of everything you have been through

I realize how fortunate I have been to have you

This day on which we celebrate our Mothers

By your side I want to celebrate YOU, MY Mother

One who has always demonstrated

All the responsibilities allocated

With this letter I hope to let you know

That you are an extra-ordinary mother

The next time she comes to visit, I surprise her with her gift. As she reads it, tears roll gently down her cheeks. She expresses appreciation and simultaneous regret, "Mija, please forgive me." I'm more than shocked and humbled by her words. They immediately soothe me and I can't help but respond with, "Forgive me, mamá." We give each other a long hug. It's as if with her loving words she reaches deep inside me and heals the wounds I could not touch. I feel my heart rest in hers. Deep in our hearts we're both grateful for a second chance. This marks the beginning of the eventual healing of our relationship.

CHAPTER 6:
MOVING FORWARD

After our long hug, my mom looks around the room and helps me gather my personal belongings. It has been two weeks and I'm able to go home. I go through the necessary process of being discharged and I'm wheeled out. My wheelchair is placed in the truck and I'm helped in. We drive away. It's the first time I've been outside of the hospital in two weeks, and the first time I've been to Santa Rosa, California. Since I didn't see it on the way in, I'm curious about what it looks like. As we drive away from the hospital, I notice the beautiful homes, buildings, and small boutiques. I enjoy the sunlight and activity on the streets. It has the feeling of a quaint and quiet town. I feel a sense of vulnerability as we drive away from the place that held me in its embrace and cared for me since I arrived.

On the way home, we stop by the wrecking yard where my crashed car is being held. I need to pick up a briefcase full of important paperwork and documents that I was carrying the day of the accident. I'm in awe when I catch the first glimpse of my wrecked car and instantly remember what it looked like before the accident.

My beautiful Honda Accord is destroyed. I can't believe how bad it looks. It feels surreal to see it but looking at it confirms the reality of the accident. Not that it didn't feel real when it happened, but seeing the shape it's in, really makes it all come together. This mangled piece of metal gives me the message loud and clear. We will not be going home together.

I can't stand to look at it for long. I want to gather my belongings and put this experience as far behind me as possible. I take the pictures you see and ask my mother to help me empty out the glove compartment, the console, and the trunk. She asks for some shopping bags from the wrecking yard's administrative office, and stuffs everything into them. We drive home in complete silence. This brief pause in my life is over. It is time to move forward.

Upon arriving home, my mother suggests that I camp out in the living room so I can easily ask for help when needed. She already has the hide-a-bed prepared with clean sheets and blankets. There is no television in this room, so I must find other ways to pass the time. This isn't too difficult since I'm pretty accustomed to being without it. We didn't have a television while I was a small child in Mexico. My early memories of television consist of walking by one of the neighborhood homes and noticing everyone huddled up in front of a thirteen-inch set. It looked claustrophobic and joining them was not an attractive thought. Instead, I spent my time outdoors playing games with the neighborhood kids.

I ask my mom to bring me books from my bookshelf and any others she thinks would be good for me. She brings mostly self-help and motivational books but along with them is also a Bible. I submerge myself in the volumes I had for some time intended to read, but for one reason or another, had not gotten around to it. The stories help keep my mind entertained and in a positive state.

Life at home slowly gets back in rhythm. It is late morning and my brothers and sister are away at school. My mom is out running errands. The need to go to the restroom hits me instantly, and in my haste to transfer myself to the wheelchair, I lose control and momentarily forget not to bear weight on my feet. The sharp pain that shoots up my leg instantly reminds me as I see the floor coming towards my face. I put my hands out in front of me to soften the fall.

The house is quiet. All I hear is the sound of my own breathing. I look around wishing somebody was here. I observe myself from an onlooker's perspective and imagine what a pitiful sight I must be. I remember the countless times I strolled into a nice restaurant with a beautiful dress draped around my legs. I attempt to fight the tears of self-pity that are welling up.

After recovering from the humiliation of the fall, I reach for the wheelchair. It rolls out of my grasp as I attempt to grip it and I fall once again. I realize the importance of being emotionally strong because when it really comes down to it, no one is responsible for our wellbeing, physical, or emotional, but ourselves. This thought gives me a boost of strength to try again but since both of my feet are injured, I'm unable to bear weight on either one. I struggle to pull myself up with my arms while bearing weight on my knees. I'm unable to get back in either the wheel chair or the bed. After trying with all the strength I have left, I fall back onto my stomach and give in to the tears which are now rolling down my cheeks. I feel completely helpless and alone.

I'm just gaining control of my emotions when my brother's concerned voice startles me, "What happened? Are you okay?" Before I respond, he instinctively leans down, picks me up, and helps me back into the chair. I'm surprised to see him, "I didn't know you were here." He tries to avoid letting me see the sadness in his eyes. I can tell it hurts him to see me like this, so I give him an understanding smile as he quietly leaves the room.

I feel much better after he exits. I went from feeling completely powerless and pitiful one moment, to feeling soothed and able the next. Feeling the strength and support of his arms made me feel cared for. This helps me realize how important we all are to one another.

As the days turn into weeks and the weeks turn into months on the hide-a-bed, I remember that I've always thought it would be wonderful not to have to work. To have unlimited time off seemed like a dream, but I'm now seeing that it's not fun at all. The endless hours tick by in slow motion. Time seems to stand still. I'm losing track of it. One day seems no different from the other. Saturday is the same as Monday. Six in the morning is the same as six in the evening. I feel like a caged lion. The healing is coming along slower than I anticipated. I remember my doctor smiling when I told him I would be running again in six weeks.

The tingling sensation circulating through my body brings me back to the present. I'm growing restless, I want to move and express my physical energy. I feel it stirring within me. It yearns to be released. It's like an itch somewhere deep in the recesses of my gut that wants to be scratched. The only way to reach it is through physical movement. I'm so used to exercising every day that this stillness is suffocating me. I want to scream! I have to do something quick.

Memories of how good it felt to be in the gym make me yearn to be there once again. I wish I could exercise as I once did, but my feet are still in recovery and my doctor's orders not to bear weight on either one are still in effect. In an act of desperation, I drop from the chair onto my knees and do some push-ups. The instant relief I feel gives me so much joy it's difficult to contain it. It feels satiating to let the energy circulate through my upper body. I'm finally scratching the itch I couldn't scratch. I absorb the goodness flowing through my veins.

Although slow as possible, the process is moving forward. I'm now sitting on an exam room bed waiting for my surgeon to look at my right foot which has just had the cast cut off. My big toe is itching. I reach down and scratch it and a thick piece of dead skin comes off! I continue picking and more skin comes off! It's now coming off in thick layers! It's making me nervous, but I can't stop. I want to see when it's going to stop.

"Calm down and stop picking." My mom sitting next to me, gently scolds me. The doctor walks in and seeing the expression on my face explains, "It's normal for dead skin to accumulate over the months that you've been unable to wash your foot." He takes a good look at it, "The bones are healing well. A nurse will be in shortly to show you how to care for this wound. Let's schedule a follow up visit in two weeks and see how it's going." He exits the room as the nurse walks in to bandage my wound.

Once at home, I have a difficult time washing it and removing all the layers of dead skin. The open wound right at the base of my big toe must be kept dry. As instructed, I dry it thoroughly and re-fill it with sterile gauze. I'm amazed at how much gauze fits in the hole. It must be about twelve inches long. I subdue my queasiness and finish by wrapping the entire foot with protective bandages.

My next visit approaches quickly, and I'm back at my doctor's office. He unravels the bandages and takes a long, concerned look, "This wound hasn't changed from the last visit. We may have to perform surgery to close it. Otherwise, it could become infected." The word "infected" gets my immediate attention, "What? Infected?" He responds, "Yes, and if that happens there's a chance you could lose your entire foot." Concerned, I ask, "How do you plan to close it?" He explains, "We would create what's called a flap. We would cut out a piece of healthy skin next to the wound and flip it over, on top of the existing wound." I ask him, "Why can't we just let it heal on its own?" He responds, "It won't heal on its own. Skin tissue doesn't grow over tendons. That's why it's taking so long to heal." I object, "I don't want another surgery. Can you please give me some time to try to heal it naturally?" He asks, "How do you plan to do that?" I respond, "I've read about how powerful our minds are and that we can instruct our body to heal with our thoughts." I yearn to put the information to the test. He is very hesitant but after a little more pleading he consents, "Okay, I'm going to give you until your next visit in two weeks. If I don't see a change in depth and size, I'm going to order immediate surgery."

I'm determined not to go back into the operating room. I can't see the logic of causing a new wound to heal an existing wound and beginning the healing process all over again. I see the inevitable domino effect. What if the new wound won't heal? Will we repeat the process and cut another section of my foot to create another flap? It seems like a never-ending cycle of self-destruction. Instead, I determine that I will put my faith and power to the test.

The meaning of well-known phrases from the Bible become ever so clear. For example, when Jesus Christ tells us that if we believe in him, we can do the things he does, and that greater things we can do. I understand this to mean that whatever we believe in, we can accomplish, because the power lies within us. Here I lay with a wonderful opportunity to prove things that were common knowledge to one of our greatest teachers. I embrace it wholeheartedly and vow to become healthy again.

I begin by doing visualization and energizing exercises. While lying down with my feet on top of a pile of pillows, I think of the wound and imagine it getting smaller and smaller until it closes completely. I see the image on the screen of my mind as I send conscious energy to my foot by repeatedly squeezing and releasing it as hard as I can. Squeeze and release. I imagine the beautiful, pink, healthy tissue weaving itself like string and grafting onto the tendon. I see it done, the process is complete, and I'm looking at my already healed foot. It looks healthy just as it used to be. This causes me to feel a sense of joy as if I'm really seeing my already healed foot. I consciously enhance the joy by using substitution. It is an acting technique I learned that strengthens our faith and sense of reality for a current experience, by transferring the feelings from a remembered experience. I remember a moment in my life when I felt true authentic joy right in my gut. I allow myself to feel it again by reliving the memory of the experience. I now transfer this fresh surge of joy to the image of my already healed foot. I see the image while I focus on the joy and expand it until it is radiating from within my solar plexus. I realize that I'm consciously allowing my healing and bringing it into the present, and I am ever so grateful.

At my next visit, my doctor is very surprised to see the changes in the wound. It is now significantly smaller. "What did you do?" He asks incredulously. I explain, "I visualized my foot and-" He interrupts me with his hand in the air and says, "Never mind. Don't tell me. Whatever you did, just keep doing it." I smile with the understanding that from his perspective, he doesn't believe in things unproven scientifically. All that matters to me is that I'm having a miraculous healing experience.

It has now been five months since the accident and the pain medication is making me sick. I've been taking it every four hours since released from the hospital. I feel physically ill and the thought of taking another dose makes my stomach turn. It controls the pain and helps me sleep but I've also been taking muscle relaxers to alleviate the spasms and anti-inflammatories to reduce the swelling. Since these are causing symptoms, I'm now being prescribed medications to counteract them. A total of seven medications are sitting on the coffee table. The signs of the inevitable revolving cycle of illness and disease are staring at me. The warnings on the medication instructions frighten me, "I can't keep taking these." The mere thought of ingesting more hydrocodone makes me nauseous. I've also heard that it's addictive, so I finalize my decision to begin the weaning process. I know it will be very difficult, but I must take a strong stance on this.

To ensure my success, I have to find a productive way to fill my time. I'm still wearing bandages on my right foot which is supported with an orthopedic boot. My left foot is now fitting into a loose tennis shoe. Since I'm finally able to start getting around on crutches, I decide to take commercial, film, and television acting classes at the local city college.

It's a beautiful day in September. I'm hopping along on my crutches down the open hallways, immersed in the energy of the campus. I see the students' obvious anticipation of the great things they are imagining for their futures. The look in their eyes tells me they're eager to change the world.

My classroom happens to be in a portable trailer with a ramp that I'm struggling to scale as I coach myself, "Slow and steady, slow and steady." I move cautiously, staying intently focused on my task. I'm sure there must be glances in my direction but it doesn't matter. It feels good to be moving around.

I find a seat and class begins. I'm listening to the professor discuss how accents are created when I feel the pain that has been with me for the last three days, intensify into an excruciating migraine. I would love to lay my head down on the desk. The throbbing is difficult to endure since I haven't been able to sleep. I rub the back of my neck desperately trying to subdue it. The sharpness is unrelenting. I know that succumbing to the medication will make it go away. For a millisecond, I consider taking it again, but I immediately imagine the domino effect. I won't give into it. I have already endured three days and I won't waste the effort already expended. I need to hang in there, desperately.

I do not want to disturb the class, so I quietly do some breathing exercises. I begin counting to five as I breathe in. I hold my breath for a count of five and then exhale for a count of five. I can see and hear the professor, but his voice becomes muddled as I go into a relaxed state. Suddenly, I feel a warm explosion at the base of my skull, the exact point where my head ends, and my neck begins. It blasts and immediately spreads up the back of my head, down my neck, through my shoulders, and down my spine. A wonderful feeling of joy accompanies it. I can't believe what is happening. It feels magical! I want to stand up and shout about it to the class, but they would obviously think I'm crazy, so instead, I silently soak in the goodness. I allow my body to absorb and savor the deliciousness. When it stops, the headache is gone, completely gone.

I'm astonished by this occurrence. I wish I could tell everyone about the mysteries being revealed to me through this amazing journey. Never in my life have I experienced such proof of the power that sustains and heals us.

CHAPTER 7:
LETTING GO

A few days later I meet with my personal injury attorney. He has determined that the driver at fault is a young man of twenty-five years old without assets. While sitting in his office, he explains, "Although you're entitled to sue him, you will likely not receive benefits because all he owned was the truck that caused the accident. Your only recourse is to file a lien against his future assets." I'm interested in knowing more so I ask, "What do you mean file a lien against his future assets?" He explains, "This means that whenever he buys a house or anything of substantial value in the future, you can force him to sell it and compensate you."

I imagine this young man of twenty-five playing financial catch up, feeling the way I have felt my entire life. I see him struggling financially while suffering the residual effects of the mistake he made, which would inevitably spread into his family and home life. I see myself going through the intricacies of a court battle, from consultations with my attorney regarding filing motions, to preparing for and attending court appointments. This would inevitably consume me with angry thoughts and feelings of victimization which could continue to feed on each other indefinitely.

It's clear that I would have to mentally, verbally, and emotionally support my actions of suing him, which would inevitably make me the new perpetuator of the situation. With my anger, resentment, and need for retribution, I would create more suffering. With my new knowledge that thoughts and emotions have creative power, I realize that this process would create similar experiences by drawing me to other people, things, and events having similar traits. The ripple of emotions could continue indefinitely and lead me to an infinitely revolving cycle of negative thinking, actions, and reactions. This could also place me in danger of losing sight of where the originating point was, and I would get completely lost in my circumstances again. Ultimately, it doesn't matter what happened in the past, what matters is what happens NOW. The originating point of creation is always in the present.

This foresight happens in a matter of milliseconds while sitting in front of my attorney. I feel a murky feeling in the pit of my gut. It creates a very unpleasant bubbly sensation that expands through my entire chest and travels up my throat. "Huh!" is the only one word descriptor that expresses how this feels. I instantly recognize this feeling and realize that I don't want to feel this way anymore. This is where I've been most of my life and especially a few months before the accident. I DON'T WANT TO FEEL THIS WAY ANYMORE!

My instinct is to turn in the opposite direction. I want nothing more to do with this nor do I want to continue recreating the same type of experiences. I want a NEW LIFE and my inner voice says that the only way I'm going to truly heal from this experience is to let it all go. I must leave it where it happened and press the re-start button on my life. It's crucial not to carry this into the future. Although the fault is clearly his and my anger would be justified, it feels wrong to claim his future assets as my own.

"Would you like me to start the paperwork?" my attorney interrupts my thoughts. I gently shake my head, "No, I don't want to do that to him. Please close the case. Thank you for your services." I execute some final paperwork and leave his office hobbling on crutches, but I vow that I will make my own way in the world. I do not need to feed off of another human being to have my needs met.

Although I don't have medical insurance, my orthopedic surgeon has continued seeing me as an out-patient on the premise that his medical office will be reimbursed with the auto insurance settlement. Now that I have received it, I call and ask how much I owe him. His response surprises me, "I'm not going to bill you for my services. I'm waiving the fees. The money will better serve you and help you get back on your feet." The word shocked is not strong enough to explain the feeling I experience as I hear his words. All I can do is express my deep sense of gratitude. This is the first time a person not a part of my family has made such a large and direct sacrifice for me.

A few days later, I receive a response to my application for financial assistance to pay my hospital bill. They inform me of their decision to pay off my balance. Again, I'm in awe. I read the letter again. I'm speechless at the generosity being expressed. I thought my application was a long shot since the total amount of the hospital bill was a little over seventy six thousand dollars. I figured that even if they offered to pay a partial amount, it would be helpful. This feels incredible. It feels too good to be true.

This is my first time having a direct experience of philanthropy and I am truly amazed that there are such wonderful organizations and people in our world. Although my physical body is severely damaged, it seems a fair exchange for these new experiences. By being able to witness such blessings, my faith is coming to life. I believe that by releasing the young man at fault, letting go of the bad thoughts and feelings, and focusing on thoughts of a good future, I am no longer blocking the benevolent force that is always working through those around us to take care of everything for us. Wonderful things are happening in the aftermath of this tragedy.

I'm finally well enough to begin going back to the gym. Since I don't have medical insurance to cover physical therapy sessions, I have to do it myself. I'm nervous and a little scared, yet I have no choice but to move forward. I change into my gym clothes, gather all my courage, and leave the house. I'm a bit uneasy since I'm not sure how my body will respond. Although I can now bear weight on both feet, I'm still having trouble with pain and balance so I'm using a cane to help me. I feel nervous about how I will be perceived walking around the gym with a cane but determined to transform those thoughts, I focus on healing. I tell myself, "I will get my body back in shape." This is more important to me than what others might think. I focus all my attention on what my body will look like when it's healed. This helps me transform the nervous thoughts and feelings into joyous anticipation.

After going into the locker room and locking up my gym bag, I head straight to the Step Master. It's a machine that is built to make you work out your legs by pushing down with your feet as though you're repeatedly standing on your toes, alternating one foot and then the other. To say it's excruciatingly painful under these conditions is an understatement. Beads of sweat are pouring down my back and off of my forehead. I don't think I've ever sweat this much. It is so painful I want to cry, but instead, I vow that I'm going to get my legs back. As tears of pain pour down my face, I keep going. "Gentle and steady," I repeat to myself. I feel self-conscious to be noticed by the people around me, but I avoid depleting my energy by not dwelling on the murky feelings this thought creates. Instead, I turn my attention back to the goal.

I continue to work through the pain by visualizing images of what I want my legs to look like again. I clearly remember the muscular definition that used to be there and internally celebrate that it is there once again. I capture the joy as if I'm really looking at my healthy muscular legs. I've read that cells and muscles have memory so I believe that since I've worked out most of my life, my muscular memory will be activated and will help me rebuild. This is the belief system I choose consciously.

As if I was standing in front of the mirror looking at my already rebuilt legs, I allow the feeling of joy to radiate in the pit of my gut. I see images of my beautifully healthy legs glistening as I jog down the beach enjoying the beautiful sun. I can almost feel the sand squeezing between my toes. How wonderful to allow myself to feel that everything is going to be okay.

CHAPTER 8:

KEY REVELATIONS

As each of our individual life stories unfold, they reveal keys that give us insight into how to live our lives successfully. The keys are revealed in different ways. Although they are revealed through different types of experiences and very often through suffering, they essentially teach us similar lessons. Through this amazing journey, I learned that we are conscious energy, that we are creators, that divinity is our nature, that forgiving sets us free, that we have the power to heal, and that the present is all we have.

Understanding these keys helped me to unlock my creative potential. I now feel that I am living in the present and looking forward to infinitely more happiness. Overall, they helped me learn how to feel happy by appreciating the experiences that every moment brings, even if they are challenging. I now understand that challenges are exercises that help us practice and strengthen our skills and determination for the upcoming tasks. I now look forward to being a conscious and deliberate creator and helping others to stop suffering by discovering the immense power that lives within them.

It's truly inspiring and exciting to have these key revelations. I have looked forward to sharing them for a very long time but it wasn't until I listened to and trusted the guiding voice within that I was able to put them together and present them.

WE ARE CONSCIOUS ENERGY

Since the day of the accident, I've wondered about the connection between the light I saw in the ocean of faces and the light that replaced my physical body. The remaining questions are, "Was the light in their eyes a reflection of the light I was radiating? Was my own light reflecting back at me through their eyes? Did I see my own reflection? Did I see my SELF?"

When I ask these questions, I feel as if I'm on the edge of discovering something amazing, but the elusiveness of this experience is still far too intangible for me to fully grasp. What I do know is that I existed, and my physical body did not. It was truly mind bending to discover that in place of my body were tiny particles of colorful light, floating and swirling in unison but without a defined form. What was even more surprising was that, although my physical body was missing, I felt present and normal. My personality and sense of identity were intact. I felt myself "standing" there, but where was unfathomable.

In my attempt to make sense of this entire experience, I referenced scientific research that found that what appears to be solid is not solid at all. All things are actually made up of moving particles and empty spaces. Everything in our physical world moves or vibrates to a measurable frequency. Molecules, which are the building blocks of matter are composed of moving particles called atoms, and atoms are composed of moving particles called electrons. Everything in our world is in a constant state of movement, or vibration. Depending on the speed of the movement or vibration, is how we perceive it with our five senses. We perceive one rate of vibration as sound, at a higher rate of vibration, we perceive it as heat, and at even higher vibrations we perceive it as light. In the center of the tiniest of these particles of matter there is an invisible force which causes the atoms to circle around one another at an immeasurable rate of speed. According to some spiritual leaders, this invisible force is the basis of our origin and everything and everyone in our physical world originates in this force.

Though my experience continues to perplex me, I believe this is a plausible explanation for the beautiful swirling light I saw in place of my physical body. Since I felt present, awake, and aware of being there, I have concluded that we are light, or conscious energy vibrating at such a frequency so as to transform ourselves into a physical form. This light shines with incredible luminosity and is who we really are.

We are a product of the fastest vibrating energy which is the basic building block of everything that exists. We are a spark of the all-knowing intelligent energy that exists everywhere. We are omnipresent because this energy exists everywhere, in everything, every being, animal, plant, and object. We are omniscient because this intelligent energy is infinite. We are omnipotent because this energy is the source and power of all that exists. All in all, we are infinite creative intelligent energy that has divided and transformed itself into each one of us.

This energy wants to express through our bodies. They are the vehicles through which we express being. The body's five senses of seeing, hearing, tasting, touching, and smelling allow us to experience our physical world. If we didn't have a body we would be deprived of the ability to interact with others and our physical environment. This is one purpose that our bodies serve.

There are experiences and desires within us yearning to be experienced. I believe that if we don't become conscious of and allow the expression and expansion of this intelligent energy through the creative expression of our desires, we feel intense pressure that causes us internal pain and we become frustrated. This frustration has the potential to become destructive as it can lead us to transform it into destructive behaviors and reactions.

In the field of psychoanalytic psychology, this energy is termed "libido." When inhibited, it is called a "repressed libido" and when directed outward onto others, it is expressed as aggression and violence. When it is completely repressed, it causes our physical bodies to become stagnant and the process of decay begins to set in. Overall, if we block our natural individual goodness and creativity from flowing, the stagnation will breed discontent, disease, and eventually completely shut down the physical body.

Our belief in aging causes us to accept these bodily changes as natural, not as what they really are, a symptom of our state of mind. My opinion is that repressing our creative energy significantly increases the process of aging by inhibiting the chemicals our bodies make to keep us young. It increases stress hormones that when produced in excess for long periods, increase inflammation in our bodies and decrease immune functioning. Therefore, aging is but the beginning of the decaying process.

When we allow our energy to circulate through creative expression and invigorating physical activity, we renew the flow of oxygen and life force to our cells and bodily functions. Our bodies respond gratefully with vigor and youthfulness. Although the years we spend on this planet continue to accumulate, our bodies continue to renew themselves at the cellular level. Scientific research has found that cells regenerate themselves automatically. Each one of us regenerates our own skin every seven days and every single cell in our body is replaced every seven years. We don't know how our bodies renew themselves throughout life, but research has shown that they do.

KEY 2
WE ARE CREATORS

I'd previously read that the power to create our lives lies within us, but somehow, the full understanding of that truth eluded me. It wasn't until this life-threatening accident that I gained clarity. During the moments between life and death, it became apparent to me that our power to create is innate.

Six months prior to my accident, my grandmother who cared for me until I was eight years old, passed away. I wasn't aware of the fatal seriousness of her illness and her death caught me completely off guard. I had taken the unexpected trip to Mexico to attend her funeral and upon returning, lost the job I had not long before acquired. Not to mention, I was at the culmination of a slow, painful break up of a long-term relationship.

It was very late, and I couldn't sleep, so I decided to go out for a drive. It was windy and chili outside. There were Christmas decorations everywhere. The tall street poles were showing off big red bows that were waving in the chilly wind. Others had beautiful wreaths hanging from them. I drove by expansive homes with large windows displaying Christmas trees. This part of town always splurged for the holidays. Although there was magic in the air, I felt like I wanted to die. I wished I could join in the holiday cheer, but the sadness was engulfing me and I didn't know how to escape it. Instead, I took Highway 50 and hit the gas pedal.

As soon as my car slammed into that tree, I remembered the powerful thoughts, images, and emotions I had on that cold winter night. I instinctively knew that I created this tragedy through the trend of thinking and feeling that I had immersed myself in for many days and nights prior to and following that night. In that moment, I clearly saw that all things spring forth from our thinking and feeling. Through our thoughts, we project the pictures that will materialize into physical expression. With our feelings we magnetize those pictures and give them the power to pull circumstances together and manifest them into material form. I finally understood what is meant by the phrase, "ask and it shall be done." The thoughts we hold in our mind combined with our feelings are "asking" and therefore, projecting our experience.

A successful experiment conducted in the 1930's that encompasses photographing thought, supports these concepts. The experiment found that pictures came out clearer when the thinker intensified their thoughts with more emotion. This experiment illustrates that our thoughts are charged with magnetic vibrational energy that is magnified by our emotions. Since our emotions or vibrational waves are magnetically charged, we are magnetic. In essence, our thoughts cause emotions which magnetically attract toward us, people, objects, and experiences that are on the same electromagnetic frequency as our emotional content. If the nature of others' thoughts is not in alignment with our own, they will not be able to associate with us. It's like trying to mix oil and water. They just don't mix.

We are the creators of our lives and together we create our earthly experience. We are the creators and the created. Now I understand how the essence of the word "God" represents the power we have to create our experience. God is conscious, creative, intelligent energy. It is what lives in us, through us, and longs to be expressed in our own unique way through creative endeavors and loving interactions with others. Our ability to use this power consciously is dormant because of our lack of acknowledgement of its existence. We walk around like beggars asking for a piece of bread when the ability and right to feast is ours.

No matter what the circumstances are, they are being held in place by our attention. If we could just believe that we could have and deserve to have the good things we desire, we would. Even if what we desire seems nowhere in sight and every thought on earth has to change to make it happen. If we can fully accept and embrace it, as if it is already ours, it will manifest. It is not necessary for us to understand ahead of time, how it will come about. All that is necessary is for us to believe.

That is the exact manner in which I unknowingly created this event. I saw images and felt incredibly powerful emotions which were later matched by this experience. Although it's clear that the young driver attempting to pass me caused the accident, I now understand that he simply served the purpose which helped to propel my passionately reckless desire into manifestation. It became clear and apparent that no one else was responsible. It was not an accident. THERE ARE NO ACCIDENTS. We define them as unforeseen and unplanned events or circumstances, but I now see that, "Everything truly does happen for a reason."

I'm so grateful to understand what that reason is. This knowledge has helped me avoid creating further tragedies in my life. I've achieved this by continuously taking my attention away from thoughts or circumstances that cause me to suffer or fear and focusing it on thoughts that make me feel good; regardless of the current reality I may be experiencing. It's helpful to remember that what we are experiencing currently is the outcome of our previous thoughts. If we want to avoid creating more of the same, we must change our thoughts. We can feel just as alive and even more vibrant with good thoughts; ones that will bring us the experience of what we really want. Whatever is not in alignment with our good thoughts will begin to dissipate on its own when we take our attention away from it.

KEY 3
DIVINITY IS OUR NATURE

Through the love and support that was expressed by Will, the paramedics that saved my life, the nursing staff at the hospital, my surgeon, and my family, I realized that our true nature is divine. Although it is hidden in some of us more than others, we all have the power to express divinity and grace. We are all angels in physical disguises.

During this most vulnerable experience when I could have met my tragic end, I found myself surrounded by angels. They were wearing the disguises of my rescue and nursing team, my family, my friends, and of every single wonderful person that served my needs during this incredible journey from near death to recovery. Through this experience, I was blessed with a glimpse of the wonderful goodness and divinity that exists within and around us.

Their expressions of love and support helped me to realize that we are all a part of a divine force that is embedded within us. Although we are individuals, we all live and exist in this force. It is a very real, sustaining, and benevolent presence that surrounds us and is always with us. Even when we are ignorant of it, for it is our own essence, our own being. I believe that our true nature is divine, pure, and perfect. We just have to open up to it and allow it to express itself through us. This can be accomplished by tuning ourselves into thoughts that inspire feelings of love, joy, and appreciation on a regular basis. The types of thoughts we have cause us to vibrate at their congruent frequency. Thoughts that make us feel good make us vibrate at a faster frequency, more like that immeasurable divine force which is the source of our being.

Thoughts that make us feel bad cause us to vibrate at a slower frequency which is less similar to that force.

This is why we feel so good when we allow the loving energy within us to express and flow to one another. It is because we are vibrating at the rate or frequency that is higher and closer to our divine nature. Through the choices we make, we express our divinity. For example, my nursing team chose to make a living saving people's lives, thus they were there when I needed them. My rescuer, Will chose to put his early morning destination aside to assist me, and thus helped save my life. Their thoughts and choices were expressed through their actions and their actions expressed the love and desire to serve. I believe this defines divinity, for to be divine means to be virtuous, and the desire to help others is a virtuous quality. Ultimately, we are all here to serve each other. It is love and divinity trying to express itself through each one of us. We just have to allow ourselves to feel it, allow the service to be provided, and be grateful for the service we receive. Supporting each other allows our natural goodness to flow. Not only does it make us feel good, it heals us, and promotes a more humane and loving Earthly experience.

There are examples of divinity all around us. Just look at a baby girl or boy that has been fed and nothing hurts. They radiate the most pure and perfect, innocent sweetness. The joy in their eyes is beyond divine. We have so much to learn from the pure joy they so naturally and easily express. We don't have to do much to bring it out of them. A simple "peek-a-boo" will make them burst out in what I call "gut" laughter. It is real and authentic. The sound of their high-pitched squeals bring joy to our ears. They are so happy to be here on earth that they're always ready to express it. The reason they bubble with joy at every opportunity is because joy is what they are. They are joy and love in the flesh. However, through conditioning, they learn how to desire things outside of themselves and temporarily forget that they already are everything they desire. They grow up and forget what they came here to do, and that is to share their gifts and talents by expressing and enjoying them through these disguises called "bodies."

We can find the divinity in others by looking past the masks we have fabricated with depressing, worrying, and angry thoughts. These types of thoughts cloud our divine image. They cause us to frown and thus cover up the beauty and joy that is natural to us. Let's look past the masks by remembering that each of us is a divine being. We are made up of pure love. We're wearing a temporary mask because we have temporarily forgotten our true nature. When we look past the masks and smile genuinely at everyone we come in contact with, we shine a spark of light upon them that has the potential to help them remember the joy that is natural to them. They may even shine a smile right back at us.

Psychologists have discovered what they've termed, mirror neurons, which they describe as the ability to mirror in ourselves what someone else is feeling. These neurons are a type of brain cell that responds equally when we perform an action and when we witness someone else perform the same action. Based on this discovery, we can understand how a smile could be contagious. As we walk around smiling, others will mirror us and the people they come in contact with, will mirror them. As in a domino effect, we can surmise that a single smile has the power to spread throughout the entire world and make everyone smile.

This research could also explain how we obtained our masks. If from early childhood we watched others suffer, we naturally mirrored their behavior and body language and after enough mirroring, learned how to suffer. The pure and perfect innocent sweetness (our divine nature) we were born with was incrementally covered up. The discovery of mirror neurons could help parents support their children when sad events occur. For example, the loss of a loved one can bring great pain. Children may witness the pain in others and mirror it. During these moments we can support our children by explaining to them that it's natural for them to mirror how others feel. If they experience being hurt by what someone else did, we can help them deal with the pain by explaining to them that we are all here to enhance and facilitate each other's Earthly experience. We do this by filling the roles we need each other to fill so that we may have the experiences we desire. We could not enjoy the dramas of life if we were completely alone.

Every moment brings us an experience that allows us to learn more about life, and ourselves. As long as we are alive, we will have experiences that will lead us to more personal understanding and growth. Thus, giving us the ability to make choices that are more in alignment with what we really want to experience. We need a variety of experiences to help us understand our own likes and dislikes. The variety is what gives us the ability to appreciate. We cannot truly feel what joy feels like, if we've never experienced sadness, because we would not have a basis for comparison. It's okay for us to feel sad feelings momentarily, but we can help our children change their perspective by helping them remember the joy that is natural to them. This can be accomplished by remembering happy experiences or by pointing out some of the beautiful things around them.

KEY 4
FORGIVING SETS US FREE

I now understand that a primary reason my mother and I couldn't get along while I was growing up was because, by the time she brought me to the United States to live with her, I was too consumed with blame, resentment, and anger towards her. I pretty much blamed her for everything that went wrong in my life. What initiated the healing of our relationship was a shift in the thoughts I was placing my attention on.

It's very easy to lose track of what came first, the thought or the experience and blame our experience for our thoughts, but this is a sure way to get stuck in the revolving cycle of self-destruction. If we blame the experience, we not only avoid responsibility, we lose our power to change our circumstances. Instead, we create destructive thought patterns which cause us to feel unpleasant emotions. These emotions then cause us to react in ways that perpetuate the existing conditions.

It is not our personal responsibility to see that justice is served. Let's give credit to our intelligent Universe and understand that life has its own way of bringing justice. Everything that exists has intelligence in it. We don't have to exert our personal energy by holding others responsible or attempting to change them, or the events associated with them. It wasn't by accident that we ended up with the families, friends, co-workers, and circumstances that make up our lives. We were magnetically attracted to them because they were most likely to provide us with the environment to grow in the specific areas necessary to continue our evolution.

When we blame others, we essentially fence ourselves in with unpleasant thoughts. We hold ourselves hostage because we are the ones experiencing our unpleasant thoughts about them. We exert a lot of energy holding on to thoughts of that which we are not forgiving. When we forgive, we release ourselves from our own mental and emotional grip. We free ourselves from the attachments we have to painful memories, thoughts of future possibilities, emotions, regrets, and expectations regarding a person or event.

In order to have the ability to forgive, it will help us to understand how we are contributing to the creation of everything that happens in our lives. This will allow us to accept responsibility for our part of the experience. Whether we do it consciously or unconsciously, we are the creators of everything that happens in our lives. We are responsible for our thoughts and feelings, our choices and our actions. Our attention, intentions, and desires create an energetic blueprint of the subject of our attention. When enough attention is continuously placed, the blueprint is established, and it magnetically attracts the entities or circumstances that share similar desires or vibrational traits. This is how by "coincidence" people come together for a similar purpose. This is also how circumstances are created to give us what we focus our attention on. It is our own attention to these circumstances that is holding them in place. We are the ones fueling them with our own power. As if our very attention was holding them in suspended animation, when we take it away, the circumstances dissolve.

Knowing this can help us be compassionate with ourselves and others by allowing us to move past the blame and accepting that we all did the best we could with the information, energy, resources, and knowledge that was available to us at the time. If we knew and had then, what we know and have now, we would probably have made a different choice. The expression, "Hindsight is always 20/20" comes to mind, because if we look hard enough, we can usually look to the past and see very clearly what we could have done differently. Unfortunately, because the past cannot be changed, it's important to learn from these experiences and if faced with a similar situation in the future, make a different choice.

This tragic experience helped me understand that the power to change lies in the present. We can stop the cycle of destructive creation by placing our attention on what we want and taking it away from what we don't want. This is how we allow the good things we want to be expressed through us. I realized this when I stopped focusing on the negative aspects of my relationship with my mother and started focusing on appreciating the good things, she did for me. The moment I opened up my mind to her good qualities, a new path was created for us to meet halfway, and to begin the healing process. It's evident through our immediate and mutually forgiving reactions that she was longing for understanding and healing just as much as I was. Because both of us were longing to get along, our intentions and energetic vibrations matched, and we have been able to manifest a beautifully healthy, loving mother-daughter relationship ever since.

When we forgive, we let go and rise above the dimension where our difficulties exist and free ourselves from their effects. We essentially take ourselves completely out of the equation and grow into another level of awareness where these difficulties cannot exist. Forgiveness exists in a dimension of love and whenever the presence of love exists, nothing less than love can penetrate. It simply will not exist in our experience if it does not match up to love.

When we forgive, goodness begins to pour into our lives because it has been anxiously waiting for us to let it in. It was our own tight grip on the past that kept it from flowing in. The obstacles that before seemed very real begin to crumble and slowly disappear. Solutions appear from seemingly nowhere and we know that it is because we are allowing them. Through the dimension of forgiveness, faith takes precedence in our lives. Things work out for the best and even when we can't see up ahead, we feel assured that the way is already prepared. We don't worry because we know that worrying creates more of what we don't want.

WE HAVE THE POWER TO HEAL

Seeing the wound the doctor said would not heal on its own, grow smaller and smaller, as I practiced imagining the healthy tissue reproduce and attach itself to the tendon, showed me that healing is programmed into our bodies. Our job is to allow it and stop blocking it with fearful thoughts.

Through pronouncing with intense joy and gratitude, "Thank you for my healing. I am so grateful that my foot is now perfect and whole. Thank you. Thank you. I love you my beautiful foot. I love you. I love you." My foot responded to the loving energy I felt. Instead of feeling anger toward it which would have blocked its natural ability to heal itself, the love I felt caused it to respond with new healthy tissue. As the two weeks slowly passed, I noticed the wound shrinking. It was incredible. It filled me with joy and gratitude to witness the healing happening right in front of my eyes. As my visualization exercises began to gain momentum, I no longer had to use the technique called substitution to feel the joy. It began to be triggered by witnessing the conscious healing process.

This entire healing experience showed me that truly, anything is possible. I was able to transcend the physical limitations that could have kept me in a wheelchair, or required me to always be accompanied by a cane. How miraculous to witness that the human body is equipped with everything it needs for healing and wellbeing. All we have to do is believe in it, allow it, and support it. It knows what to do. We witness this happen as everyday occurrences with children banging themselves up. A cut heals itself and disappears in a week or two, but we rarely stop to contemplate how amazing that is.

We are all healers. The energy that runs through our bodies is all powerful. This energy can not only heal our own bodies, it can also heal others; as long as they believe and are willing to receive the healing. Another's faith, strength, and energy have the power to give us a boost. This is similar to giving another car "a jump." It transmits energy to it which in turn helps the other car to self-generate. I realized this when I felt the strength of my brother's arms as he lifted me from the floor onto the wheelchair. I understood something I had never before explored. I suddenly understood how much power we have and how influential and important we are to one another. His presence and strength comforted me and made me feel that everything was going to be okay. The same thing happened when my surgeon looked into my eyes. The clarity in his eyes reassured me and helped me believe that I would be okay.

KEY 6
THE PRESENT IS ALL WE HAVE

Prior to having this amazing experience, I was distinctly afraid of life and what unknown might come my way. My unpleasant, past experiences constantly haunted me and replayed themselves in my mind, causing me to be transported away from the present and to relive the pain of the past. During the moments while this accident was happening, I understood how I had been a participant. That moment itself became so overpowering, it required my full and undivided attention. I needed every bit of energy just to focus on breathing and staying alive. I was stripped of all thought about the past and the future and just experienced what it feels like to be present. It was the first time in my life that I experienced being truly conscious.

Being hospitalized and not having any obligations, I realized that the concept we call "time" doesn't really exist. It is only a man-made mechanism that measures and organizes activity or movement. We subdivide this movement into seconds, minutes, hours, days, weeks, months, years, decades, centuries, millenniums, and so on. This is how we organize our lives. We place a time stamp on everything so we can coordinate and be in sync with ourselves, with others, and with our world. We use this mechanism to meet goals and objectives. We allow ourselves to become slaves and the slave masters are the alarms and the clocks we set to ring their commands.

When activity ceases, so does our concept of time. It becomes irrelevant when there is no activity associated with it. When there are no deadlines to meet; it doesn't matter if it's eight in the morning if we don't have to go to work. Five in the evening is no

66

longer important, if we haven't been at a job all day, longing for the clock to strike so we can go home.

In the overall scheme of life, there is no yesterday or tomorrow. Today will become yesterday and tomorrow will become today. Therefore, it's always today, and today, the only thing that exists is our awareness and the activities we participate in. Plants grow, fish swim, animals hunt, planets rotate, and we strive to know, express, and feel our own greatness. We are the motion within the infinite stillness of the present.

CHAPTER 9:
ACTIONS YOU CAN TAKE

Overall, this journey initiated my awareness of an intelligent, energetic force that permeates throughout all of life. It marked the beginning of my understanding of who, and what, that elusive force is. I have since learned that this intelligent force is our source of life and energy. It is ours to dispose of as we wish. It permeates throughout our lives and supports our point of view, no matter what it is.

Although we use this force on a daily basis, many of us do it subconsciously. When we are not aware of this benevolent force, we suffer. Much of our suffering comes from how we learned to utilize this force from an early age. We may have watched those around us subconsciously ignore, block, or misuse this naturally powerful, creative, energetic force, and thus mirrored their emotions and behaviors.

Any activity practiced often creates a habit. The type of thoughts we think become deeply ingrained within us and become habitual mental patterns. Our emotions, which are measurable physical reactions to our thoughts also become habits. Our feelings, or mental associations to the emotions we have, become habits as well. Overall, this pattern of habits becomes the operational baseline for our life experience.

Habit causes our thoughts to appear automatically. The thoughts then set off instantaneous electromagnetic chain reactions that cause things to happen, or not to happen. This can be a blessing and a curse. If our habit of thinking is laced with thoughts that cause pleasant emotions, wellbeing will be our baseline. If we allow our minds to be consumed with thoughts that make us miserable, we are likely to continue recreating similar conditions. When we focus on problems, we give them our creative energy and attention which makes them more dominant in our lives, and magnetically attracts more of them.

Until we learn how to acknowledge and utilize this innate, energetic force constructively, we will continue to feel empty and hungry inside. We will continue to believe that wellbeing and fulfillment lie somewhere in the distant future, when our conditions are perfect, and we have no more to fear. We will continue to believe in the fantasy that "one day" everything is going to be "magically" perfect and that we will have all of our desires met. I call it a fantasy because the word fantasy contains within its definition, the concept that what we are imagining is impossible or improbable. The reason it most likely is, is because we don't believe it to be true for us now. If we truly believed it now, we would feel fulfilled and it would cease being a fantasy. It would be our reality.

Fear is inherent in a fantasy. It is the dynamic that immobilizes us and keeps us from taking constructive actions to make our desires a reality. We are afraid of imagined forces working against us. We perceive these forces as real and through our belief in them we become immobilized. We are essentially influenced by our own imagination.

Nature intended fear to be constructive. The biological and chemical mechanisms that govern our emergency responses date back to primordial times. These responses helped our ancestors to protect themselves from predators and to survive. Without them, they would have been vulnerable to destruction. In modern times, the things that make us fearful are benign by comparison, but the human body's response is exactly the same whether a threat is real or imagined. The high levels of cortisol (the body's main stress

70

hormone) required during heightened moments can wreak havoc on our bodies and over time can contribute to a weakened immune system, and cause a range of metabolic disorders, including depression. When we look at the negative implications of suffering, we can easily build a case for choosing fulfillment. Ultimately, fulfillment is our goal, yet it escapes us fervently. It reminds me of the writings that compare us to the musk deer that leaps to its death off of the mountaintops while searching for the arousing scent it doesn't realize is coming from its own chest. Like the deer, we look for fulfillment everywhere except for where it lies, within our own being. It seems elusive because it is not something that is reached or created. It has always been there, awaiting our recognition, acknowledgement, enjoyment, and expression.

There are actions we can take to free ourselves from suffering and access our fulfillment. With daily practice, these actions will yield the results we yearn for. For now, let's be comforted in knowing that the feeling of fulfillment we desire is already ours. It is our true essence. We don't have to look for it or be anxious about it. All we have to do is acknowledge and feel it. It is what we already are and what we are made of. That's why we feel so connected and complete when we catch a glimpse of it. Although that may only happen when a bit of it escapes from where it is deeply hidden, under all the fearful thoughts and feelings that block it.

The first step to fulfillment is to acknowledge it. Take time to become one with it. When we do, we will find that we are that elusive, intelligent, creative force that is also the creative power of the universe. When this force is acknowledged, it multiplies our ability to execute our goals and manifest our desires. Our vision becomes clear and we begin to see our purpose. We are creative beings and we have the power to change our experiences. We can do this by taking stock or inventory of our thoughts, deciding and keeping what is good, forgiving and discarding what is not. When our thoughts are in order, we are able to create what we want consciously. Since our experience is a reflection of our state of mind, we can ultimately live in the present and feel fulfilled.

The following actions are suggested in hopes that they will introduce you to your journey through self-discovery, fulfillment, and conscious living. Each action is broken down into simple and easy steps to follow.

ACTION 1
TAKE TIME TO BE

You might not think you have to take time to be, because you are in the state of being all of the time. However, it is important to take time to become aware of being. To become conscious and feel how good it feels to acknowledge your own presence. Through the acknowledgement of your being, you will feel a sense of fulfillment and everything you go through will flow smoother. If you do it at night just before going to sleep, not only will you sleep better, but you will also be better equipped to start your day in the morning. This is because acknowledging your self satisfies the thirst you feel and replaces it with the power and confidence to handle anything that comes your way.

Step 1:   Sit

Sit in a quiet place, away from other people. Turn off your phone and all electronic devices that could disturb you. Have a note pad and pen ready so you can write down ideas that come to you. During this quiet time, solutions you have been searching for will most likely appear because you have finally quieted down enough to hear them. You will hear your inner voice guiding you. If you listen, trust, and follow, you will find that everything in your life begins to flow smoothly. Now get comfortable and turn away from all distractions. Give yourself this moment to sit still and become aware.

Step 2:   *Breathe*

Close your eyes and breathe in deeply. Exhale slowly. Allow your muscles to let go and relax. Now breathe in as you count from one to ten and allow yourself to savor the deliciousness of the air flowing into your lungs. When you get to ten, hold your breath in and count from one to ten again. Feel the warmth that begins to spread through your veins as you allow the oxygen to circulate through your body. Now exhale as you count from one to ten. If counting to ten is too long, you can count to five or any other number that is comfortable for you.

This three-part breathing exercise is considered one cycle. Practice a few cycles until you experience a sense of calm and peace, then allow your breathing to ebb and flow naturally.

One Breathing Cycle:
- Breathe in while counting from one to ten (or five)
- Hold the breath while counting from one to ten (or five)
- Exhale while counting from one to ten (or five)

Step 3:   *Remember*

With eyes still closed, find that place within where everything is peaceful and calm. If it's a challenge due to current thoughts or circumstances, start by remembering an experience that brought you a profound feeling of love and joy. Choose a very happy memory, a time when you felt the vibration of joy deep in your heart and gut. It may be a very distant memory but no matter how far away in the past, allow yourself to remember it now.

Step 4:   *Feel*

Remember the details of the joyful experience and allow the feeling of it to permeate your being all over again. Feel it. Let it spread through your body. Pay attention to your solar plexus as you remember the feeling. Feel how it gently contracts when you remember the joyful feeling. Breathe it in and enjoy. Do not judge it, allow it to feel good for no other reason than that it's what is helping you to feel good right now. Inhale the goodness of the memory and feel it saturate your being. Take this moment to feel what it feels like to be. It feels good to allow the soothing sensation of goodness and wholeness. Take in deep breaths and truly savor the feeling of the cool air moving in and throughout your body. Realize that your body is your tool to interpret and communicate with the world.

Step 5:   *Acknowledge Yourself*

Notice that the feeling of joy is not attached to the memory anymore. It's vibrating in your gut right now. Can you feel it? Let it vibrate through your gut. Savor it. This good feeling is who you really are. This is the feeling that has been on standby, waiting to be felt and expressed. Since the day you were born, this feeling accompanied you. It's what bubbled out of you with glee when your mother and father held you in their arms and played with you. It's what was constantly waiting for any excuse to laugh and giggle with glee. Anything to spark it into expression. Though life's trials may have clouded your memory, this wonderful feeling of goodness is who you really are.

Step 6:   *Be Grateful*

Be grateful for this opportunity to acknowledge and be yourself. Being grateful tunes us into the flow of goodness in our lives. When we express gratitude, we acknowledge the greatness of the power that sustains us, provides for us, and is us. It acknowledges the presence of the good in our lives. When we acknowledge the good, we unleash it.

ACTION 2
TAKE INVENTORY

If being doesn't feel good right now or you find yourself unable to reach a state of calm, take inventory. Look at your life and assess everything; relationships with others, living conditions, employment, goals, dreams, desires, and anything else that is of high importance to you.

The first step to consciously redirecting our lives is to assess our thoughts. Assessing them allows us to identify the ones that are causing us to feel bad and the ones that are causing us to feel good. Once we identify them, we will be able to organize them and put them in their proper perspective. This will give us the peace of mind necessary to enjoy being in the present.

Repeat steps 1 and 2 from Action 1 and continue through the new steps described.

Step 1:   **Sit**   (refer to *Action1* for details)

Step 2:   **Breathe**   (refer to *Action 1* for details)

Step 3:   **Observe**

Pay attention to your thoughts. Allow them to flow freely. Watch them as they flash through your mind. Let them flow as they want without judgment. As you observe, concentrate on your solar plexus and heart area. Notice how you feel when you have a thought. Continue paying attention to all of the thoughts that ebb and flow through your mind. Notice how your feelings change as the thoughts change. These feelings are indicators of your preferences.

Step 4:   *List & Keep*

Write down every thought you have and draw two columns under it. In one column describe what is pleasant about it and in the other column describe what is not. Do this in as much detail as possible. This will be your guide to deciding which thoughts in your current experience are in alignment with your sense of wellbeing and which thoughts are not.

Now read your list of thoughts and everything you wrote in the columns under them. As you read, circle the thoughts that inspire good feelings. These thoughts you will keep. Whenever they spring into your mind let them flow freely. Appreciate them and allow the good feelings they inspire. We will look at the ones that feel unpleasant in the next action.

ACTION 3
FORGIVE

Forgiving is the greatest act of self-love we can engage in. This is because when we forgive, we stop resisting our own wellbeing. When we have unpleasant and resentful thoughts about ourselves or someone else, we, by default, block ourselves from feeling good. We, as the thinkers, experience their effects. We feel bad, and by feeling bad, we create what is called resistance. This resistance blocks us from receiving the good things we desire.

To help us understand the concept of resistance, let's imagine that it's a sunny day and we are sitting next to a body of water, breathing easily and freely. This rhythmic breathing represents the good feelings that are natural to us. Now imagine that you jump into the water and forcefully hold your head under it. Even as the innate urge to breathe tugs and pulls within your chest, you resist it and continue to forcefully hold your head under water. In a similar way, when we concentrate on thoughts that make us feel bad, we forcefully resist the good feelings that want to be felt.

When we forgive, we feel lighter because we have released the weight of our resistance. Our outlook changes and we see with more clarity, direction, and purpose. With continued practice, our life becomes peaceful, meaningful, and free of suffering. This new state of wellbeing simultaneously puts our life in order. All of the good things we have been wanting begin flowing into our life because we are no longer resisting them.

The process of forgiving involves a few easy steps that are described in this section. Every time you feel disturbed by unpleasant thoughts, repeat them. If you practice releasing negative thoughts on a consistent basis, the time will come when you will no longer feel the need to feel resentful. You will know that thinking unpleasant thoughts goes against your own wellbeing and you will release them.

Begin by repeating steps 1 and 2 and continue through the new steps described.

Step 1:   ***Sit***   (refer to *Action1* for details)

Step 2:   ***Breathe***   (refer to *Action 1* for details)

Step 3:   ***Analyze***

Review the list you created in Step 4 of Action 2 and focus on the thoughts that gave you unpleasant feelings. Look at the first thought and allow the corresponding feelings you feel as you think it. Then read all of the unpleasant thoughts on your list. If these thoughts inspire resentment toward yourself or something someone else said or did, let's prepare to release it.

In order to do this successfully, it is important to analyze where the resentment came from. It is possible that when you heard words being said or experienced actions being executed by someone who lacked the ability to communicate constructively, you had an unpleasant emotional response. This response was your way of knowing that what you were experiencing was not in sync with your wellbeing. If you became angry following the emotional response, you, by default, chose to be resentful. Over time, the inability to release this anger bound you in your own resentment, confusion, obsessions, and unhealthy desires.

Step 4:   ***Accept***

Now that you have a better understanding of where the resentment may have come from, you are on your way to releasing it. However, first you must accept it. To do this, it may help to accept that people who use offensive words and act in hurtful ways, do so, because *they* are hurt. They don't know how to deal with their own pain and suffering. Another thing that may help is to remember that words and actions are means of communication. They are not embedded with corresponding feelings although we tend to associate feelings with them.

Look at your state of being and accept that this is where you are right now. Everything that has happened in your life has brought you to this moment. Allow yourself to be it, accept it, love it, or not, but love yourself regardless. You did your very best, even though at times you may have been able to do better. Know that you are all there is and everything there is, is you.

If you can accept your resentment, you can release it and forgive. You may even feel compassion for the person who hurt you because the very fact that they misuse their words and power to act, tells you that they lack the skills to communicate effectively. They essentially have no other means of communication. As one of our greatest teachers once said, "Forgive them Father, for they know not what they do."

Step 5:   ***Release***

Now that you have accepted your resentment, ask yourself if it is something you want to release from your life. If your answer is a truthful yes, then allow yourself to feel the resentful feelings and acknowledge that you are now consciously choosing to release them. Read the following statement out loud:

"I accept myself just as I am right now. Everything I have experienced has made me who I am today. I have always done my best, even when I may have been able to do better. I forgive myself for not trying harder when I could have. I did the best I could under the circumstances.

Life is made up of experiences. Each brings something new to make the next better. Each brings new ideas and feelings that give me a glimpse of who I am and what I prefer. I am grateful for my experiences for they have helped me to learn about my own desires and preferences. I know more about myself now than I did before them. What has already happened cannot be changed, but all of the power lies within me to change the experiences that I have yet to have. Knowing all of this, I release my resistance to the goodness that is natural to me by releasing this resentful thought.

I no longer allow you to take precedence over my life. I RELEASE you and I set MYSELF FREE. I am FREE and I am grateful for this TRUTH. I am well and complete. I am FREE. Thank you. Thank you. I am grateful for my FREEDOM. I embrace my FREEDOM NOW. I walk forth completely FREE."

ACTION 4
CREATE CONSCIOUSLY

Creating what we really want to experience can be challenging because it involves taking a close look at our preferences. We're so used to doing what is expected of us, that we rarely explore our own desires. The most important question is, "What do WE really want to experience?"

To answer this question, we must turn our attention away from what we think others want for us and towards what we want for ourselves. To tap into our creative nature, we must imagine ourselves having or living experiences we think we will enjoy. As you imagine yourself having these experiences, pay attention to how you feel. Our feelings are indicators that let us know. Basically, if it feels good, it's the direction we should go. If it feels bad, it's not.

Step 1:   Write

Write out a description of the solution, outcome, or creation you would like to see. Be very specific with vivid details. Don't worry about how it will come, just figure out what you want. This can sometimes be the most difficult step because it requires much introspection and honesty. While you're doing this, momentarily suspend all doubt and fear and assume that you can have anything you want. Forget the problems because continuing to focus on them will strengthen and create more of them. Let's focus only on the solutions because they are what we desire to create. We cannot manifest the solutions if we're focused on the problems.

Step 2:   *Imagine & Feel*

Imagine having the experience, solution, outcome, or creation you have written down. See every aspect of every detail as if it was happening right now. Take time to really see it in your mind, as if it was right in front of you. See the color, size, brand, environment, weather, etc. Whatever aspects apply in your specific scenario.

Our emotions have the electromagnetic power to manifest the desired results. How we feel usually comes from the type of thoughts we have. Since the thought of what we want to create is good, let's feel good about it. Our feelings go out from us in electromagnetic waves. These waves have a corresponding vibrational frequency to the feelings we are experiencing. Whatever frequency goes out will automatically attract its corresponding physical equivalent, thus causing the things we're thinking about to happen. Through the real feelings of love and joy, we magnetize the good things and experiences we want toward us. As we imagine the outcome we desire, let's attach those great feelings to it, as though we are celebrating that it's already done. This is how we "believe" and by repeatedly believing, the desired outcome will appear. The key word here is, "believe." We must believe that our desires are possible for them to come to fruition, because we are the ones creating them. We cannot expect to create something we don't believe in.

Allow the good feelings these images provoke. Let yourself be filled with love and joy. These kinds of feelings are the ones that you've experienced in your happiest moments.

Step 3:   *Substitute*

If you have trouble feeling the love and joy that the imagined experience will bring, try the technique I mentioned previously called substitution. Transferring the feelings of a remembered experience or event, will help strengthen your faith and sense of reality for the current situation or experience. In other words, remember a time when you experienced incredibly satisfying feelings and pretend that the desired outcome you are imagining has already happened and is giving you the same good feelings. If you break down the word pretend as "pre-tend" it can be defined as, "to tend to it before it happens" and through "pre-tending" it, it happens. Therefore, pretend that you have what you want and that you feel incredibly amazing about it. Let yourself actually feel this feeling.

Step 4:   *Be Grateful*

Verbalize in your mind or out loud the following statement or something similar:

"Thank you. Thank you. Thank you. I am so happy and grateful now that _____*(describe the desired goal or outcome)*_____. *"* For example, *"…now that I have obtained my college degree in business administration."* Finish by repeating and feeling the essence of the words, *"Thank you. Thank you. I am so grateful."*

As you say these words magnetize them with the "feelings" in your gut. Allow yourself to truly feel grateful that your desire is fulfilled. It is done. Fill yourself up with satisfaction and gratitude.

After this exercise, relax and know that you have done your work. Your actions will be propelled by the work that you do internally. Do this at least in the morning and at night before going to sleep. The more frequently you do it, the quicker you will begin to believe it and take the actions required to step into the experience. When you truly believe it, you will see it happening, and your faith will be strengthened. That's when greater things will come into your experience.

ACTION 5
LIVE IN THE PRESENT

Many of us walk around consumed with our thoughts rather than paying attention to what's going on in front of us. By doing this, we miss out on the events and things that are making up our present experience. What tends to make us feel unhappy are our own thoughts about something that has already happened or that we fear will happen in the future. If we're always focused on our thoughts, we're not really experiencing what's happening in the present.

Step 1:   *Stay Aware*

As you go through your day, stay aware of what's going on around you. Put out of your mind any thoughts or images that transport you to another time and place. Stay aware of where you are physically and mentally; and be mentally where you are physically. Place your attention only on what is right in front of you. For example, are you next to a river, a lake, or in a room? If it's a body of water, what does the water look like? Is it clean or dirty? Can you hear the water? Is it still? Can you see a reflection? If you're in a room, why are you there? Are you standing in a line waiting for something? Are there other people in line with you? If so, what are they doing? Is somebody speaking to you? What are they saying?

Step 2:   *Redirect*

If your thoughts transport you to another place and time, as soon as you become aware that this has happened, redirect your attention back to the present. This can be done by immediately taking notice of the details in your environment as described in the previous step. Remember, the present is the only reality.

Step 3:   *Notice & Appreciate*

Notice the details without judging them. Be a silent observer. Notice the beauty that exists all around you. The expression of beauty is natural to life. When you pay attention to it, you will notice that everywhere you look there is beauty to be appreciated and the more you appreciate it, the more of it you will notice. Look at nature's beautiful mountains, rivers, trees, and flowers. Look up at the beautiful sky and moon, how alive they are. Everything that exists has beauty, intelligence, and life. Look at everything and everyone as a unique expression of life and drink of the goodness as a dry sponge soaks up liquid.

CHAPTER 10:
POETIC EXPRESSION

In attempting to describe the elusiveness of the concepts learned throughout this incredible journey, I leave you with the following poems which are an attempt at capturing the feelings of faith, clarity, and fulfillment that I am grateful to say are now a part of my day. I am grateful for having this opportunity to share my experiences with you. I hope that they will serve as a catalyst for your conscious health, wellbeing, and realization of your dreams and desires.

"When Faith Opens Up"

It's like a thick wall of fog

Around the invisible part of our minds

It's dark and very difficult to define

Its luring quality causes self-doubt

It causes us to lose confidence

In what we dream about

It's like an invisible monster

Grips us so tight we get flustered

We feel an exasperated frustration

It's difficult to point out its location

Then we turn it all around

We turn up the smile

Turn down the frown

The fogginess begins to clear

The problem has been solved

We can stop shedding these tears

We step into the moment

When we're living the dream

No longer dormant

Everything that was once a thought

Has to our experience been brought

It is now, it is clear, no more fear

It all seems so logical and simple

Then we realize

That wall of fog that seemed so real

Was an illusion

It created so much confusion

What is, what will be, or not

Now I know it is just a thought

"Freedom of Thought"

When human interaction stops
All we are left with is our own thoughts
The mind is not our master
Allowing it to run wild causes disaster
We choose the thoughts we entertain
From any thought we can refrain

We have an eternal choice of thoughts
We can think happy or angry until we get lost
The freedom to choose is all ours
We can inhale its essence like smelling the flowers
The sum of our thoughts becomes our life experience
Every thought to itself causes adherence
When we witness life's human interactions
Our thoughts reveal our reactions
Therefore we are only subject to our observations
We are not subject to any force outside ourselves
We can choose our thoughts from within heaven's shelf

"Tears of Joy"

They trickle down my face as one by one they go
As I feel that joyful feeling that makes me glow
It's that heavenly feeling in my heart
That one that lets me know we're not apart
It lets me know that Thou and I are One
It lets me know that Joy I have become
Some may be blinded and cannot see
That we can all express our Joy through Thee
But in time all shall see
That only love will set us free
They will all finally know
That God expresses through us all

Through time I must admit
That my faith has been put to the test
But now I know I can put my fears to rest
Now I know that I my troubles cannot defeat
For so long I've searched and searched
For that Joy that only Thy presence brings
I used to think that day would come
When all would seem clear and done
But now I know today is that day
That day when Joy is all mine

Along the road my vision was unclear

I was confused thinking Thou were nowhere near

But now I know that my Joy has not strayed

Because within me, it has always laid

To express the love that's been revealed in my life

Is to know that with God there is no strife

To see my strength be put to the test

Is to know that I am

That place through which God's beauty can reflect

How can it be that when we least expect

Our dreams will become manifest

"Divine Destiny"

When we're traveling along our divine destiny
We meet those that will facilitate our journey
In this world that seems full of chaos
They are there to help us with our cause
They're there when we least expect
God's love and protection they manifest
Like angels they're there to take away fear
They're there our path to clear
Just when we may feel a little defeated
They're there to give us what we've needed

There was a time when I didn't know
Others would be there to help me grow
If I hadn't done it, I would never have known
That if I shot for the stars
I would receive support to get so far
Others would be there to lend their strength, their faith
For me to make this trip
To the land where dreams are made

From the moment I walked through their doors
I was given a place to call home
I was exhausted

My journey had taken me into the night
But I knew when I got there it would be alright
I had the faith to believe
Faith gave me the courage to breathe

On the street I met those that wander
They looked at me with eyes in wonder
They didn't realize that although I look like I have it all
I really have so far to go
Amongst them I might seem like a queen on a throne
But to those that have accomplished much more
I'm nothing but a pauper looking to get out of being poor
But really it's not money that drives me so far
It's really my desire to reach for the stars
It is love in its pure essence that makes me live
It is love to others I want to give
That is what gives me exactly what my soul needs

Through the example that others have set
I vow to my soul that I will never forget
As long as I live, I will serve those that are in need
This I will do to thank others for their great deeds

When I'm thirsty
There's always another holding out a big glass of water
When my feet are sore
Someone is there their strength to restore
When my head is tired from the day's work
A soft pillow is there to take away the hurt

Wow! With joy I can really shout
Now that I know what God's great family is all about
Of this human race I am truly amazed
There is so much beauty on which we can gaze
Now I know no matter where I go
My Earthly people's love will flow

Life can be such a mystery
But the mysteries lie in our own mind
If we just open up we will find
That essence we call God is in each one of us
All we have to do is realize
God is Love, God is Joy, God is US!

Made in the USA
Middletown, DE
16 January 2023